WHS

NATIONAL TESTS
practice papers

FOR THE YEAR **2005**

Science

Levels 3–8

AGE
13–14
Key Stage 3

practice papers

Contents

Page

First published in 2005
exclusively for WHSmith by
Hodder Murray,
a member of the Hodder Headline Group
338 Euston Road
London NW1 3BH

Text © Hodder Murray 2005

All rights reserved. Apart from any use permitted under UK copyright law, no part of this publication may be reproduced or transmitted in any form or by any means, electronic or mechanical, including photocopying, recording, or any information storage and retrieval system, without permission in writing from the publisher or under licence from the Copyright Licensing Agency Limited. Further details of such licences (for reprographic reproduction) may be obtained from the Copyright Licensing Agency Limited, of 90 Tottenham Court Road, London W1T 4LP.

Author: Terry Hudson

Impression 5 4 3 2 1
Year 2006 2005

Printed and bound in Spain

A catalogue record for this title is available from the British Library

ISBN 0 340 88876 8

NOTE: The tests, questions and advice in this book are not reproductions of the official test materials sent to schools. The official testing process is supported by guidance and training for teachers in setting and marking tests and interpreting the results. The results achieved in the tests in this book may not be the same as those achieved in the official tests.

The National Tests: A Summary

What are the National Tests?

Children who attend state schools in England sit National Tests (also known as SATs) at the ages of 7, 11 and 14. Those at ages 11 and 14 are taken at the beginning of May. Those at age 7 can be carried out at any point during the year, as chosen by the teacher. Children in Wales may take the same tests at 11 and 14 respectively. All children may also sit optional tests in the intervening years – many schools have chosen to adopt these tests.

The test results are used by the school to assess each student's level of knowledge and progress in English and Maths at Key Stage 1 and English, Maths and Science at Key Stages 2 and 3. The results also provide guidance for the student's next teacher when he or she is planning the year.

The educational calendar for students aged 5–14 is structured as follows:

Key Stage	Year	Age by end of year	National Test
1 (KS1)	1	6	
	2	7	KEY STAGE 1
	3	8	Optional Year 3
2 (KS2)	4	9	Optional Year 4
	5	10	Optional Year 5
	6	11	KEY STAGE 2
3 (KS3)	7	12	Optional Year 7
	8	13	Optional Year 8
	9	14	KEY STAGE 3

Timetable for 2005

Key Stage 3 students will sit their tests on **3–6 May 2005** (but check with the school as dates may change).

Levels

National targets have been set for students' results in the National Tests, as follows:

LEVEL	AGE 7 (Key Stage 1)	AGE 11 (Key Stage 2)	AGE 14 (Key Stage 3)
8			
7			
6			
5			
4			
3			
2 2a 2b 2c			
1			

- BELOW EXPECTED LEVEL
- EXPECTED LEVEL
- ABOVE EXPECTED LEVEL
- EXCEPTIONAL

What can parents do to help?

While it is never a good idea to encourage cramming, parents can help a student to succeed by:

- Making sure he or she has enough food, sleep and leisure time during the test period.
- Encouraging him or her to practise important skills such as writing, spelling and mental arithmetic.
- Telling him or her what to expect in the test, such as important symbols.
- Helping him or her to be comfortable in test conditions, including working within a time limit, reading questions carefully and understanding different ways of answering.

Science at Key Stage 3

Success in the National Tests

You can improve your marks in Science by taking into account the following points:

The language used in the questions

1 The examiners will not put any useless information in a question. If something is written down then the examiner wants you to use it.
   - **Example:** *Space probes have shown that there are* ***mountains****,* ***dry river valleys*** *and* ***volcanoes*** *on Mars. Scientists believe Mars, like Earth, has all three types of rock:* ***igneous****,* ***metamorphic*** *and* ***sedimentary****.*
   You will need to use all the terms.

2 Use the mark scheme to tell you how many points you should include in your answers.

3 Read the question very carefully.
   - **Example:** *Tick the correct box.* Only tick ONE box. If you tick more than one box, the question will be marked incorrect.

4 Don't be put off if you encounter unfamiliar material. You will know enough science to answer the question. In the example above, you may not know much about Mars. However, the work you have done on rock formation on Earth will allow you to answer the question.

Key words in the questions

1 **Choose** from a list of words. Make sure you use words from the list. Unless the question states otherwise, you can use words more than once. Similarly you don't have to use them all.

2 **Describe**… You do **not** have to explain anything; you simply have to make a physical description of a diagram, graph, etc.

3 **Explain**… You need to include a scientific explanation for your answer. Include some key scientific words in your answer.

4 **Predict**… There are two possible types of prediction:
   - Predicting what you think might happen in an investigation.
   - Extrapolating a graph (continuing a trend) to predict what might happen for higher or lower values of a variable.

5 Be aware of **negatives**.
   - **Example:** *Give the name of another metal,* ***not*** *in the table…*

6 **Advantages and disadvantages**. To be on the safe side, make sure you state both in your comparisons.

7 **Name**… **Which**… **What**… **Give**… These are simple command words which require a simple response. These are often found with numbers or words in bold type.

Sitting the practice tests

These practice tests are designed to help you get used to test conditions. When you take the National Test in May you will be given an exact time **(1 hour)** and be expected to work in silence with no books and no one to help you. That is exactly how you should practise.

1 You need a pencil or pen and a watch or clock.
2 Ask someone to time the test so that you have exactly 60 minutes.
3 If you cannot read a scientific word then someone can read it to you. That person should not tell you what it means.
4 Do not start answering the questions until you have had a look at all of the test paper. This will give you a good idea of what is covered in the test and how many questions there are.
5 Read each question carefully and follow the instructions.
6 Do not spend too long over any one question. Answer it and move on.
7 If you can't answer a question, don't worry. Move on to the next one. You can always come back at the end.
8 Try to use all the time available. If you think you have finished, go back and check every answer.
9 At the end of the time, check your answers with the mark scheme and work out your total.
10 Make a list of the questions you did not do too well on, but congratulate yourself on those you answered well.
11 Discuss the questions you found most difficult with a parent or a teacher. It is a good idea to check your notes to make sure that the topic won't cause problems again.
12 After a few weeks, try the questions again. You will improve your score if you have been working and revising and you will be well prepared for the real thing.

Sound

1 Louise is caught in a thunderstorm. She sees the lightning before she hears the thunder.

a Which travels faster – light or sound?

1

b Study the bar graph below.

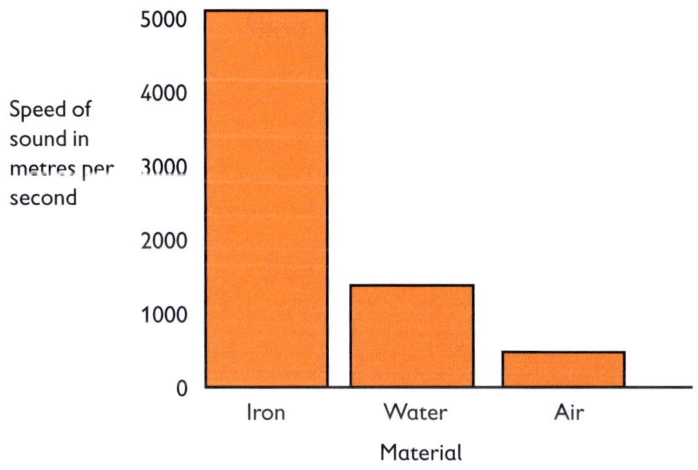

i Through which material does sound travel the slowest?

1

ii Through which material does sound travel the fastest?

1

iii Use the data to explain why tapping noises on metal pipes can be heard over long distances.

2

TOTAL

5

Cells

2 The drawings below show an animal cell and a plant cell.

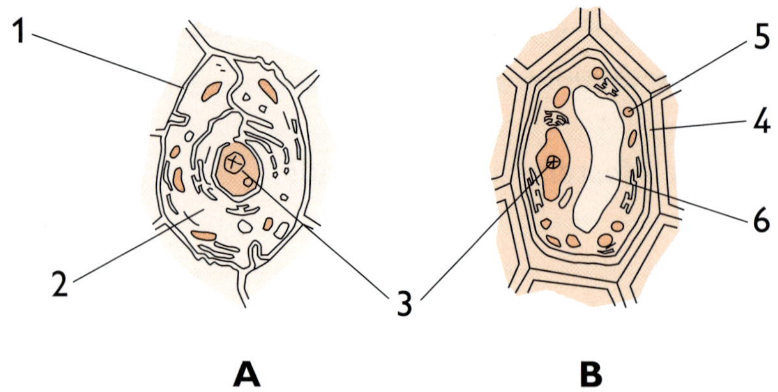

a Which of the two cells is the plant cell?

1

______

Explain why you have chosen this cell.

1

______

______

b Name the parts labelled 1–6.

6

1 = ______ 4 = ______

2 = ______ 5 = ______

3 = ______ 6 = ______

TOTAL

8

c Write down **two** differences between plant and animal cells.

i ______________________________ 1

ii ______________________________ 1

d Green plants use energy from the Sun to help them to make food.
What is the name for living things that can do this?

Tick the correct box.

herbivores ☐

producers ☐

carnivores ☐

predators ☐

1

e Describe **one** way in which plant cells are adapted to help them to use energy from the Sun.

____

____

2

TOTAL

5

Food chains and food webs

3 The drawing shows a food web in a river.
Use the information in the drawing to answer the questions.

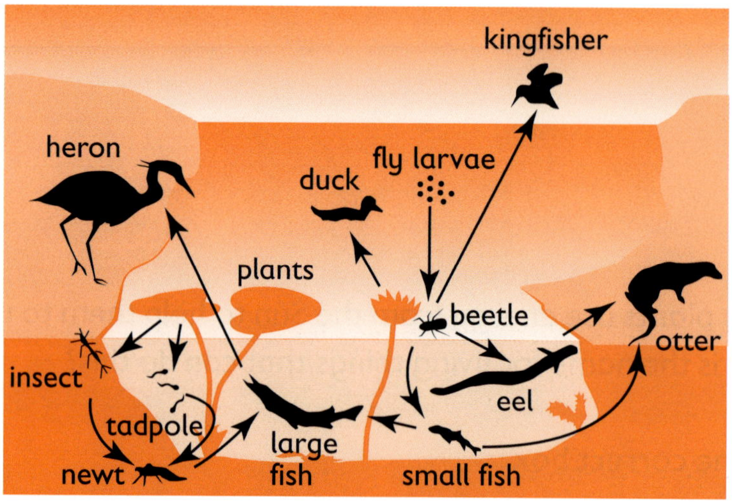

a Complete the food chains below by using examples from the river food web.

5

i plants → __________ → newt

ii __________ → beetle → __________

iii __________ → __________ → heron

b Write the name of **one** predator in the river food web.

1

____

TOTAL 6

c If all of the eels are killed by disease, what is likely to happen to the number of beetles?

____

____

____

1

d If all the fly larvae are killed by disease, what is likely to happen to the number of small fish?

The number of small fish is likely to ______________________

because ____

____.

2

TOTAL

3

Plants

4 The drawings below show two experiments to investigate the effect of light on plant growth.

Experiment 1

Experiment 2

a Which plants are the most likely to receive the most light?
Tick the correct box.

Those in Experiment 1 ☐ Those in Experiment 2 ☐

1

b List **two** factors other than light that could be different between Experiment 1 and Experiment 2.

i ______________________________

1

ii ______________________________

1

c Why is it important to make sure that these other factors are the same in each experiment?

____

____

1

TOTAL

4

d Only three plants are used in each experiment.
Why would it be better to use many more plants?

2

e List **two** different ways that you could compare how well the plants in Experiments 1 and 2 have grown.

i 1

ii 1

f Predict **two** differences that you could see between the plants in Experiment 1 and the plants in Experiment 2 after 7 days.

i 1

ii 1

TOTAL

6

Solids, liquids and gases

5 The drawing below shows a pot of tea being made.

a **i** Name **one** part of the drawing that shows a solid.

____

1

ii Name **one** part of the drawing that shows a liquid.

____

1

iii Name **one** part of the drawing that shows where a liquid has changed state to become a gas.

____

1

TOTAL

3

b The table below shows some of the properties of solids, liquids and gases. Complete the table.

property	solid	liquid	gas
volume	definite		fills its container
shape	definite	takes the shape of the container	
ease of flow		easy	easy

3

c Name **one** other property that can help to describe solids, liquids and gases.

____

1

d The diagram below shows how materials change state.

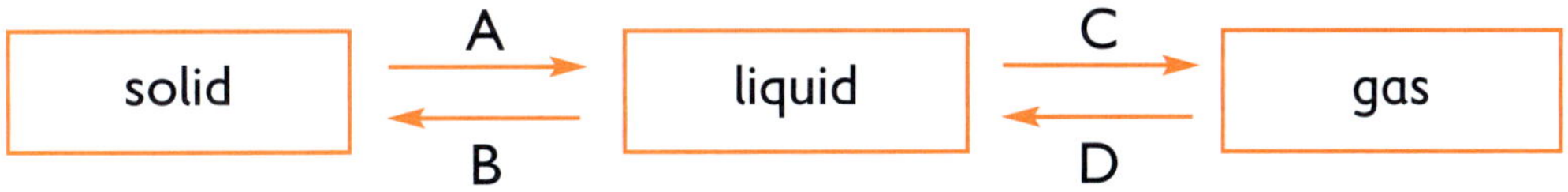

The process taking place at A is ______________________________.

The process taking place at B is ______________________________.

The process taking place at C is ______________________________.

The process taking place at D is ______________________________.

4

TOTAL

8

Testing materials

6 Steven tested a number of substances with a magnet to see if it attracted them.

a Fill in the result table. The first one has been done for you.

	Object tested	Was the object attracted to the magnet?
A	paper	no
B	copper wire	
C	steel nail	
D	aluminium foil	
E	plastic spoon	

4

b

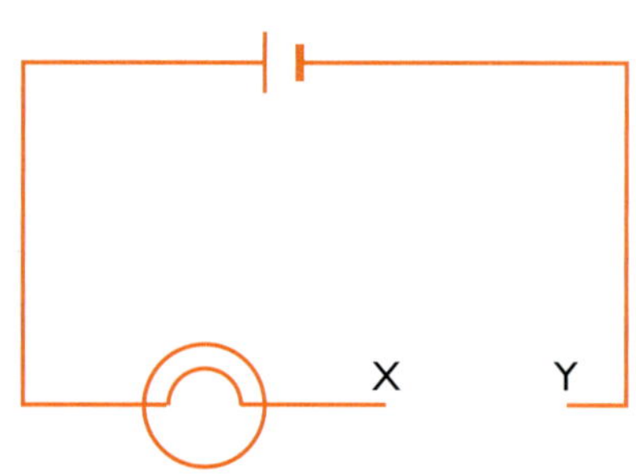

Steven connected each object A–E one at a time between X and Y in the circuit above.

i Name **three** of the bjects that will make the bulb light.

____

____

____

3

TOTAL

7

ii Name **two** of the objects that will not make the bulb light.

____

____

2

TOTAL

2

Forces

7 The drawing below shows a sledge being towed across some snow.

a There is a force pulling on the sledge through the rope. Draw an arrow on the rope to show the direction of this force. Label it A.

1

b There is also a force through the rope pulling on the child. Draw another arrow on the rope to show the direction of this force. Label it B.

1

c If the child applies a bigger force to the sledge, what will happen to its speed?

____

____

1

d Draw an arrow to show the direction of the weight of the sledge. Label it C.

1

TOTAL

4

e The picture below shows a parachutist falling.

i Draw an arrow on the diagram to show the direction of the force of gravity acting on the parachutist. Label it A. 1

ii Draw another arrow on the diagram to show the direction of the force due to air resistance. Label it B. 1

TOTAL 2

The Sun and the Earth

8 Helen lives in the north of Britain.

a Where does the Sun rise in the morning?
Tick the correct box.

in the south	☐	in the west	☐
in the north	☐	in the east	☐

1

b Where does the Sun set in the evening?
Tick the correct box.

in the south	☐	in the west	☐
in the north	☐	in the east	☐

1

c At what time of day is the Sun highest in the sky?

____

1

d Explain why the Sun seems to move across the sky.

____

____

1

TOTAL 4

e The diagram below shows the Earth and rays of light approaching it from the Sun.

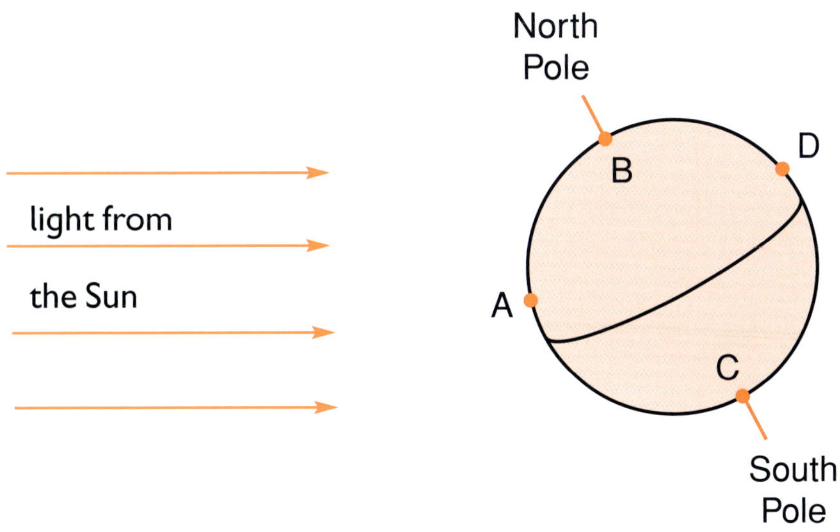

Write down the letter of the point which matches each description below.

i It is light here for 24 hours a day at this time of year:

____________________ 1

ii It is dark here for 24 hours a day at this time of year:

____________________ 1

iii It is midday at this point:

____________________ 1

iv It is night-time at this point:

____________________ 1

TOTAL 4

Circuits

9 Thomas and Sylvia have made up three circuits. They are shown in the diagrams below.

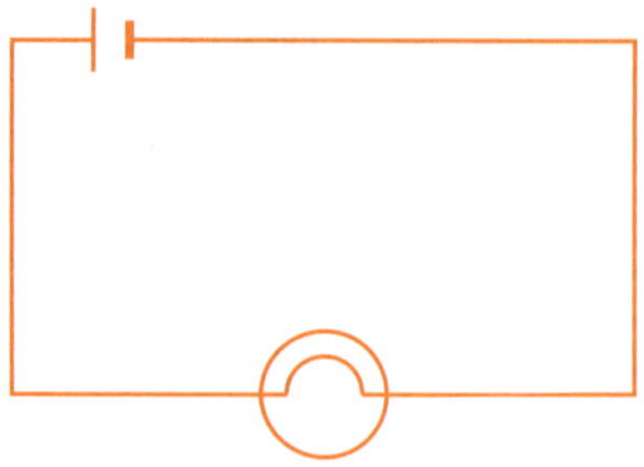

A

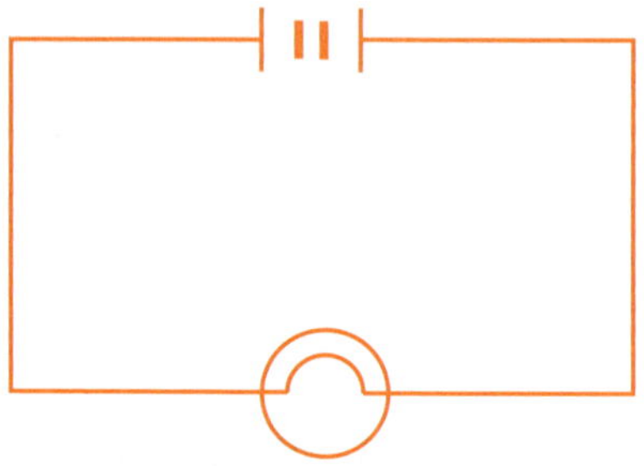

B

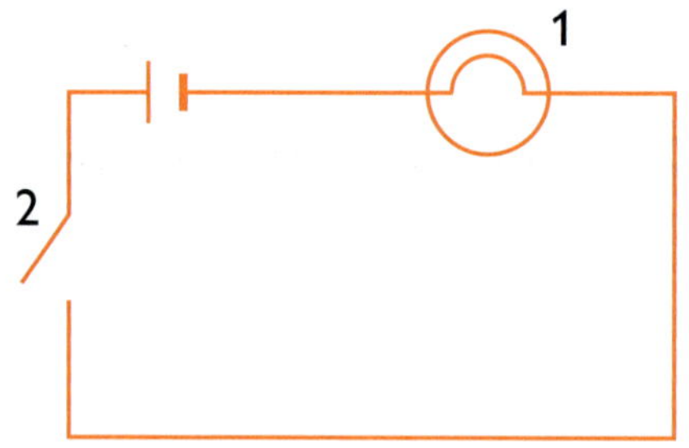

C

a Write down the names of the two components numbered in circuit diagram C.

Component 1 is ______________________.

Component 2 is ______________________.

2

TOTAL

2

b In which of the circuits will the bulb light up?

____

1

c Thomas and Sylvia close the component labelled 2 in circuit C.

Will the bulb light up? ________________

1

Explain your answer.

____

____

2

TOTAL

4

Nutrition

10 Fat, proteins and minerals are three types of nutrients found in foods.

a Give the names of **two** other types of nutrients needed for a balanced diet.

i ______________________________

ii ______________________________

2

b A balanced diet must contain a variety of foods.

i Describe **two** reasons why a balanced diet **must** contain protein.

____

____

2

ii List **two** important uses of fat.

____

____

2

iii Give **two** reasons why a balanced diet should not contain too much fat.

____

____

2

iv Name a disease caused if vitamin C is missing from a balanced diet.

____

1

TOTAL

9

11 The diagram below shows part of the human skeleton.

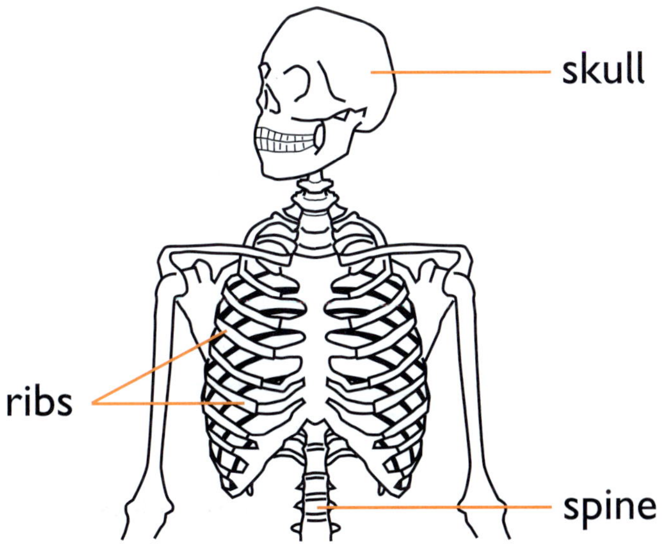

a Write down the name of the part of the skeleton which protects the brain.

______________________________ 1

b Write down the name of the part of the skeleton which protects the heart and lungs.

______________________________ 1

c The spine must be strong, but must also be able to move so that a person can bend.
Describe how the spine is built to allow a person to bend.

____

______________________________ 1

TOTAL 3

d The diagram below shows the muscles that help the arm to move.

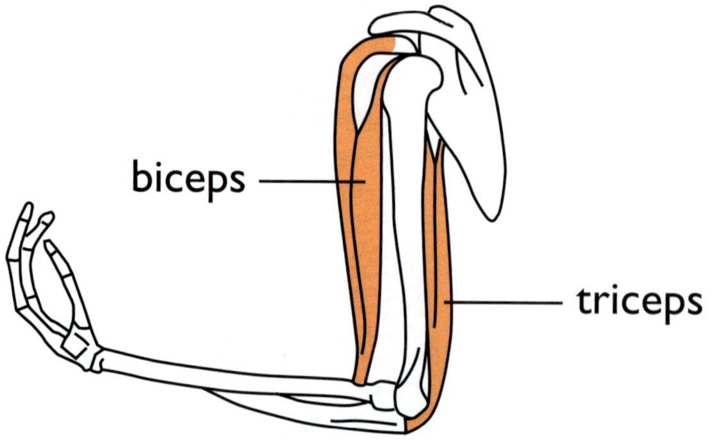

i Which muscle straightens the arm?

____

1

ii Which muscle bends the arm?

____

1

iii Explain why the arm cannot be straightened and bent by using just one muscle.

____

____

____

2

TOTAL

4

12 Stewart and Fatima have been investigating some substances as part of a school experiment. They add the substance to water and see if it dissolves. Their results are shown in the table below.

Substance	Dissolved	Did not dissolve
wood		✓
sugar	✓	
sand		✓
plastic		✓
salt	✓	

a Write down the name of **one** substance from the table that has not dissolved.

____________________ 1

b Write down the name of **one** substance from the table that has dissolved.

____________________ 1

TOTAL 2

1

c Complete the following sentence by selecting the correct word from the list.

insoluble sonorous opaque soluble amorphous

When a substance dissolves we say that it is _______________.

3

d Stewart and Fatima would like to study the dissolving of sugar in more detail and try to find out how they can make it dissolve more quickly.

Suggest **three** ways that they could make the sugar dissolve more quickly.

____

____

____

TOTAL

4

Separating mixtures

13 a The apparatus in the diagram below is used to obtain sand from a mixture of sand and water.

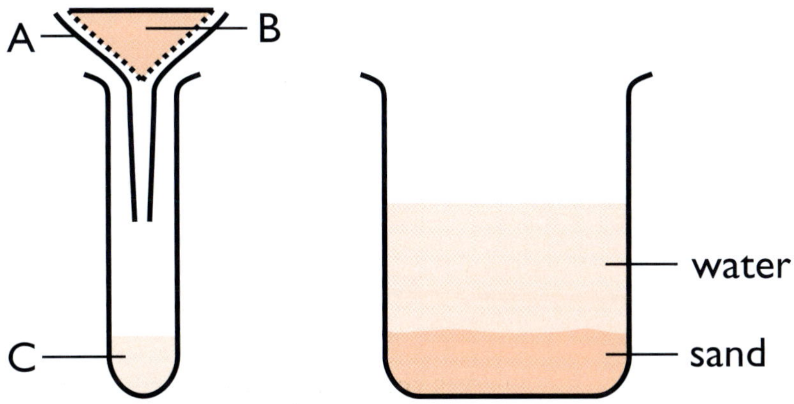

i Which substance in the diagram can be described as sediment?

______________________________ 1

ii Which substance in the diagram can be described as a solvent?

______________________________ 1

iii Name the parts of the diagram:

A ______________________________

B ______________________________

C ______________________________ 3

TOTAL 5

b Michelle is using chromatography to show which colours are present in inks. The results are shown in the diagram below.

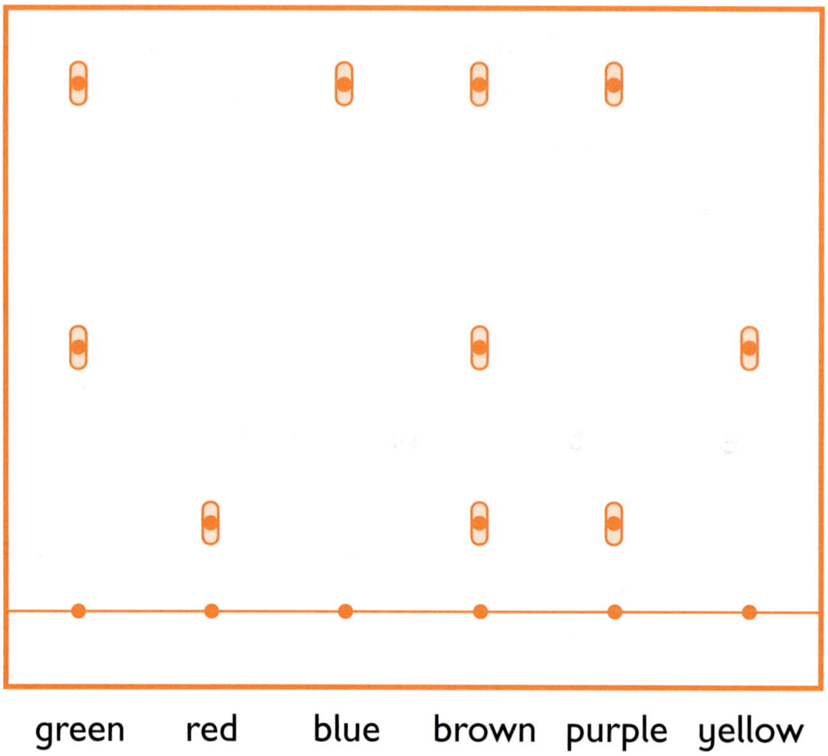

i Which ink is a mixture of yellow and blue inks?

______________________________ 1

ii Which ink is a mixture of red and blue inks?

______________________________ 1

iii Give the name of an ink which contains only one colour.

______________________________ 1

TOTAL 3

14 Amanda is investigating magnets. She is trying to see how magnets repel or attract each other.

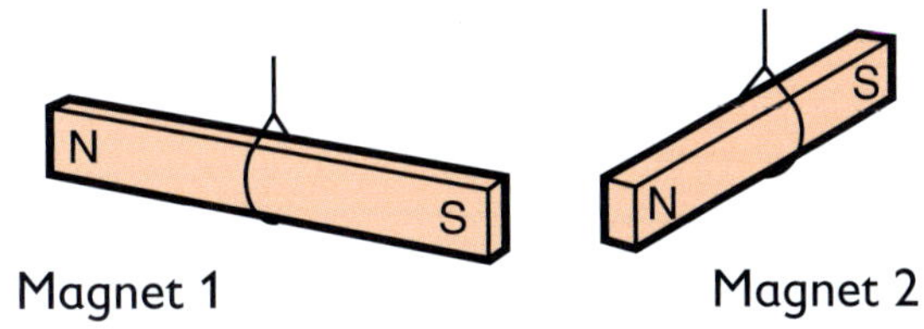

Experiment	Magnet 1	Magnet 2
A	N S	S N
B	S N	N S
C	N S	N S
D	S N	S N

a What will happen when like poles (S–S or N–N) are moved towards each other?

____

1

b What will happen when unlike poles (N and S) are moved towards each other?

____

1

TOTAL

2

c Complete the following table. The first one has been done for you.

4

Material	**Attracted to a magnet**	**Not attracted to a magnet**
lead		✓
copper		
iron		
plastic		
steel		

d Give **two** uses of magnets.

2

____

____

TOTAL

6

15a The diagram below shows the structure of a flower.

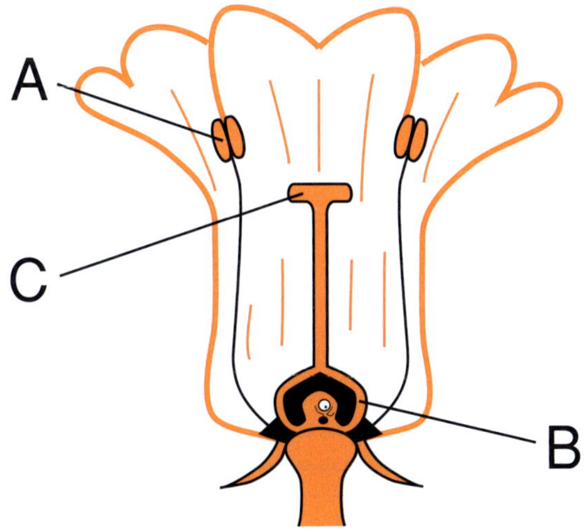

i Structure A is called the ______________________. (1)

ii Structure B is called the ______________________. (1)

iii Structure C is called the ______________________. (1)

b Complete the sentences below by choosing words from the list.

ovary	anther	stigma	style
filament	petal	wind	animals

Pollen is made in the ______________. This pollen can be spread to other flowers by ______________ and ______________. When the pollen lands on the flower it can stick to the ______________. A pollen tube then grows down the style into the ______________. (5)

TOTAL 8

Energy

16a A stretched elastic band is a source of energy. How is the energy stored in a stretched elastic band?
Tick the correct box.

as thermal energy	☐	as kinetic energy	☐
as chemical energy	☐	as potential energy	☐

1

b A car is driven to the top of a steep hill. Energy is transferred to the car as it moves higher up the hill. This energy is stored in the car while it stays at the top of the hill. What energy has the car gained?

____

1

TOTAL

2

END OF TEST 1

1 The drawing below shows a cell from a plant.

a On the diagram, label parts A, B, C, D and E.

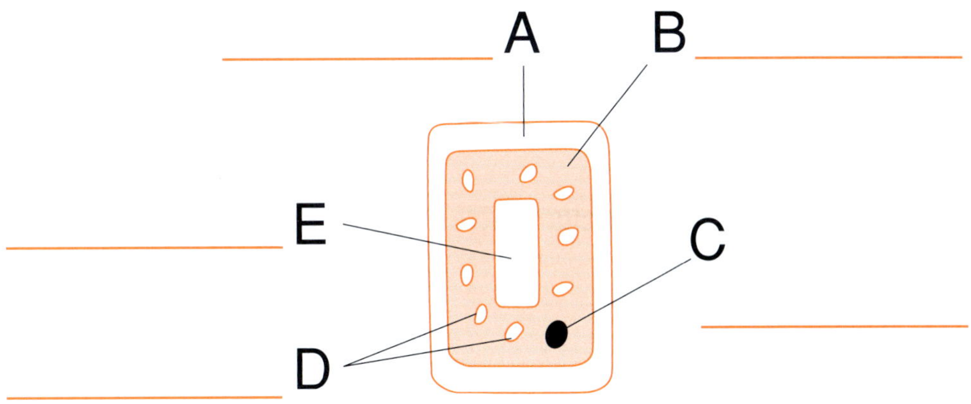

5

b In which part of a plant would you expect to see cells that do **not** have the parts labelled D?

Explain your answer.

3

c Plant cells have some parts which animal cells do not have. Name **two** of these parts.

i

ii

2

TOTAL

10

2

d Individual cells can join together to form tissues.
Write down the names of **two** types of tissues found in animals.

i ______________________________

ii ______________________________

2

e How are red blood cells specialised to carry oxygen?

____

____

____

TOTAL

4

2 The drawing below shows part of an organ system.

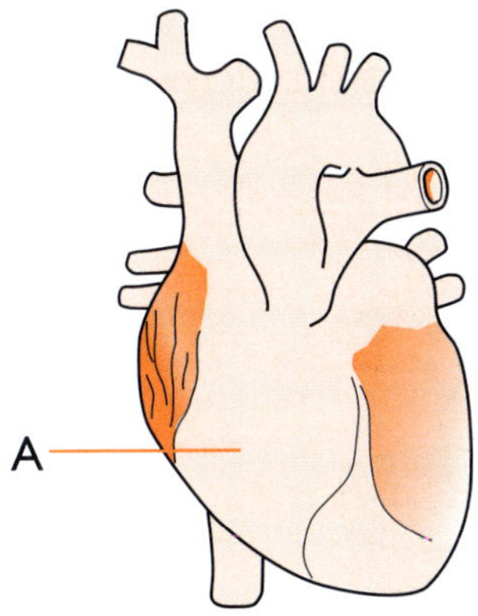

a Name the organ labelled A.

______________________________ 1

b Which organ system is A part of?
Tick the correct box.

reproductive system	☐	digestive system	☐
circulatory system	☐	respiratory system	☐

1

c Where is this part of the organ system found in the body?
Tick one box.

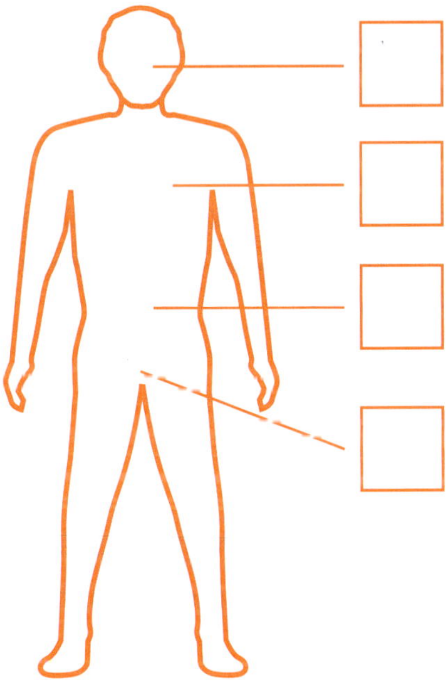

1

d List **two** functions of this organ system.

i ______________________________

ii ______________________________ 2

TOTAL 5

Plants

3 Abdul and Susan grew geraniums as part of an investigation on plant growth. At the end of their investigation they examined their plants. The diagram below shows the plants.

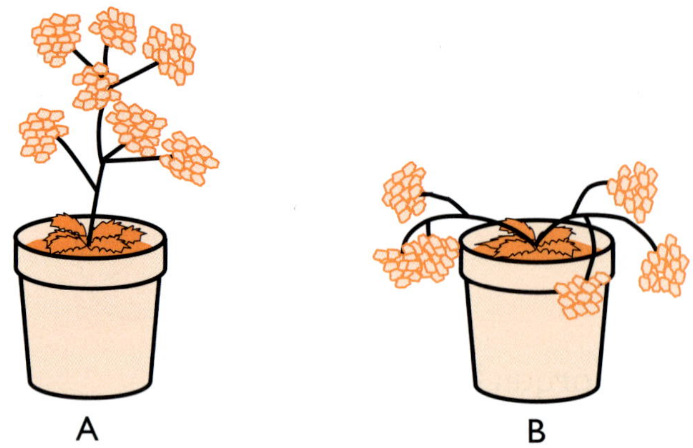

a Plant A was kept on a window sill.

Plant B was kept in a corner of a room.

Explain why being on a window sill made plant A much healthier than plant B.

____

____

____

2

b Suggest **two** factors that would have to be kept constant in order to make this investigation a fair test.

i ____

ii ____

2

c Explain why Abdul and Susan should have used more than just these two plants in this investigation.

____

____

____

2

TOTAL

6

Solutions

4 The graph below shows how the solubility of two salts in water changes with temperature.

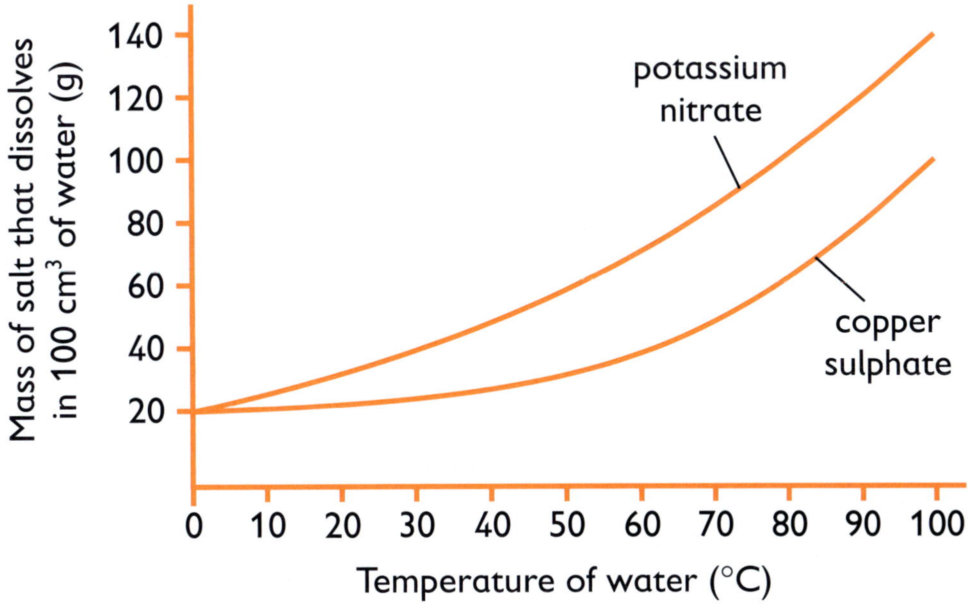

a Describe how the solubility of the salts changes with temperature. 1

____

____

b Which of the two salts is the most soluble in water? 1

____

c What is the solubility of potassium nitrate at 30°C? 1

____________________ g per 100 cm^3 of water.

TOTAL

3

d What is the largest amount of potassium nitrate that can be dissolved in 100 cm^3 of water at 50°C?

____

1

e At what temperature are the solubilities of copper sulphate and potassium nitrate the same?

______________ °C

1

f Describe **two** other ways in which you could make the salts dissolve faster in the water.

i ______________________________

____

ii ______________________________

____

2

TOTAL

4

5 The diagram below shows a volcano.

a Name the four parts of the diagram.

A ______________________________

B ______________________________

C ______________________________

D ______________________________

4

b When rocks form at A, B and D there is a change of state.
What is the change of state?

______________________ to ______________________

1

c Rocks at A cool much faster than rocks at B.
Which rocks would have the largest crystals?

____

1

TOTAL

6

d The diagram below shows a close view of the rocks deep inside a volcano.

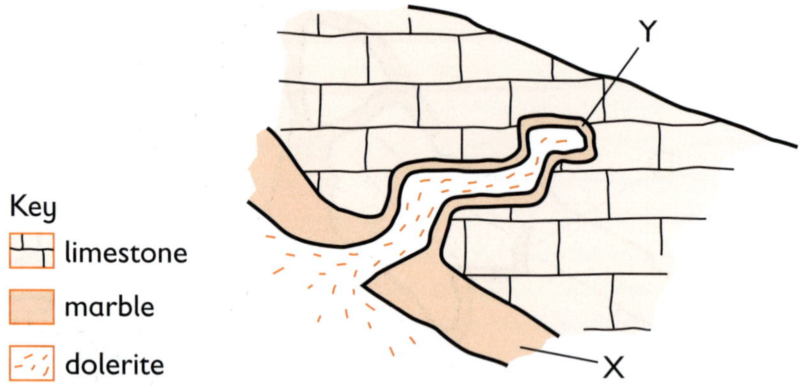

i Which type of rock is limestone? Tick the correct box.

igneous ☐ metamorphic ☐ sedimentary ☐

1

ii Explain how the limestone could have been formed.

____

____

____

2

iii Which type of rock is marble? Tick the correct box.

igneous ☐ metamorphic ☐ sedimentary ☐

1

iv Why is the marble thicker at point X than at point Y?

____

____

____

2

v In which of the three rocks would you be most likely to find fossils? Explain your answer.

____

____

____

2

TOTAL

8

6 Joanne and Naresh are shining a light from a ray box onto a plane mirror.

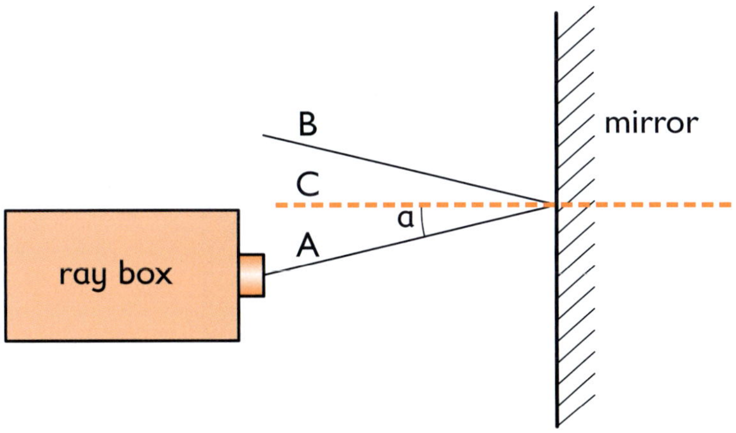

a Which of lines A–C on the diagram is the normal line?

____

1

b What is the name of angle a?

____

1

c Which of lines A–C is the reflected ray?

____

1

TOTAL

3

d Complete the following sentence.

The angle of __________ is __________ to the angle of __________.

3

e Look at the drawing below.

Why is it impossible for the person to see themselves if they stand to the side of the mirror?

____

____

____

1

TOTAL

4

7 Shabana is investigating a liquid. She adds different substances to the liquid and records her results. Her results are shown below.

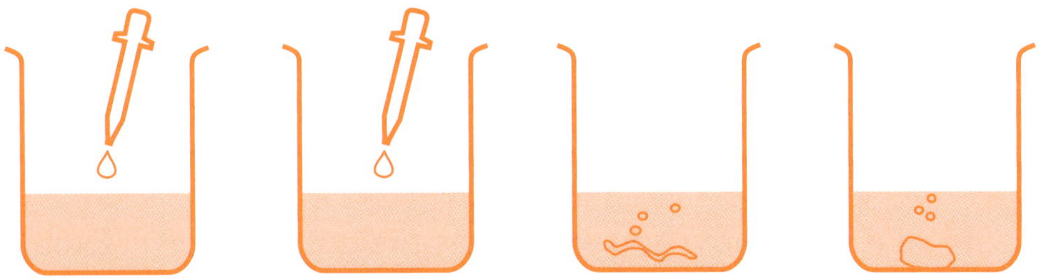

Experiment	Result
A	No colour change
B	Colour change: blue to red
C	Magnesium ribbon fizzes and bubbles of gas are given off
D	Marble chip fizzes and bubbles of gas are given off

a Is the liquid an acid or an alkali?
Tick the correct box.

acid ☐ alkali ☐

1

TOTAL

1

b **i** Name the gas given off in Experiment C.

1

ii Describe how you would test the gas given off in Experiment C to identify it.

2

c **i** Name the gas given off in Experiment D.

1

ii Describe how you would test the gas given off in Experiment D to identify it.

2

TOTAL

6

8 The diagram shows part of a food web in a pond.

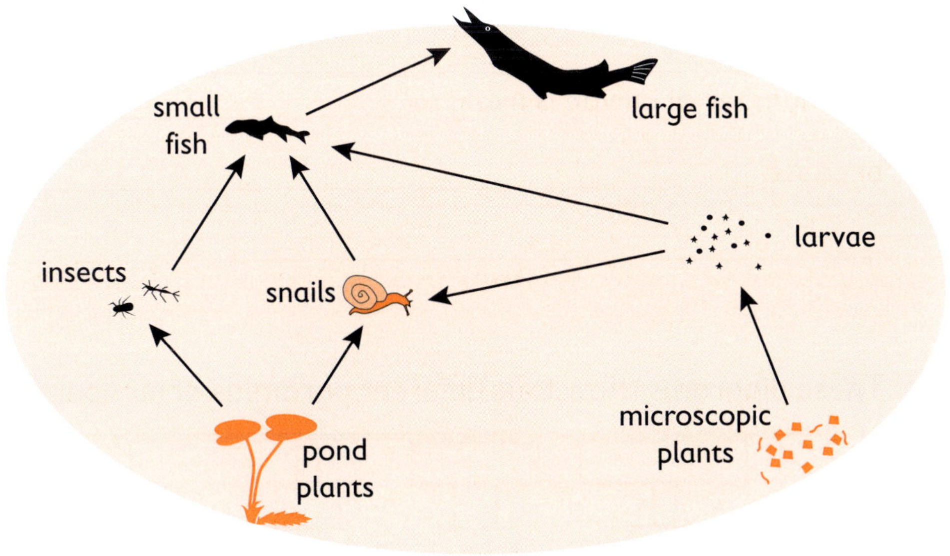

Study the food web and then answer the following questions.

a Write **three** names of living things from the food web to make a food chain.

____________ → ____________ → ____________

3

b Write the name of **one** producer in the pond food web.

____

1

c Write the name of **one** predator that has **two** prey in the food web, and the names of its prey.

Predator ________________________

Prey A ________________________

Prey B ________________________

3

TOTAL

7

d If all the microscopic plants were killed by herbicides, what is likely to happen to the number of larvae?

The number of larvae is likely to ______________________

because ______________________

______________________.

1

1

e These diagrams show four different pyramids of numbers.

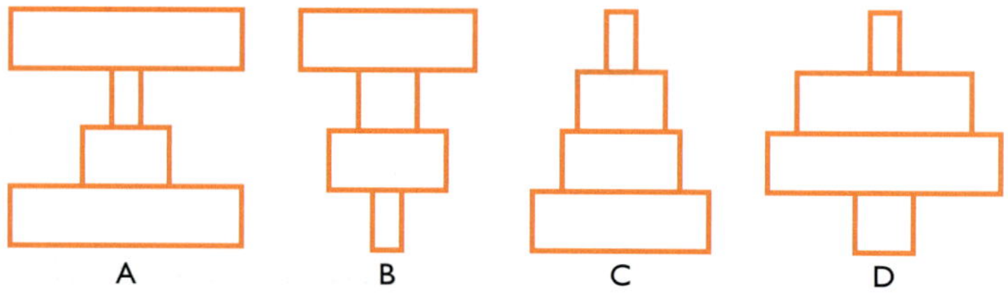

One food chain in the pond food web is:

pond plants ⟶ snails ⟶ small fish ⟶ large fish

Which of the diagrams best represents the pyramid of numbers for this food chain? ☐

1

TOTAL

3

9a The parts of a plant cell have different functions.
Draw lines to join each part of the cell to the correct function.

Part of cell	Function
cell wall	photosynthesis takes place here
nucleus	helps to keep the shape of the cell
cytoplasm	a place where many chemical reactions take place
chloroplast	controls substances entering and leaving the cell
cell membrane	controls the cell's activities

5

b Plant cells use carbon dioxide in photosynthesis. The graph below shows the amount of carbon dioxide absorbed by a plant during one day.

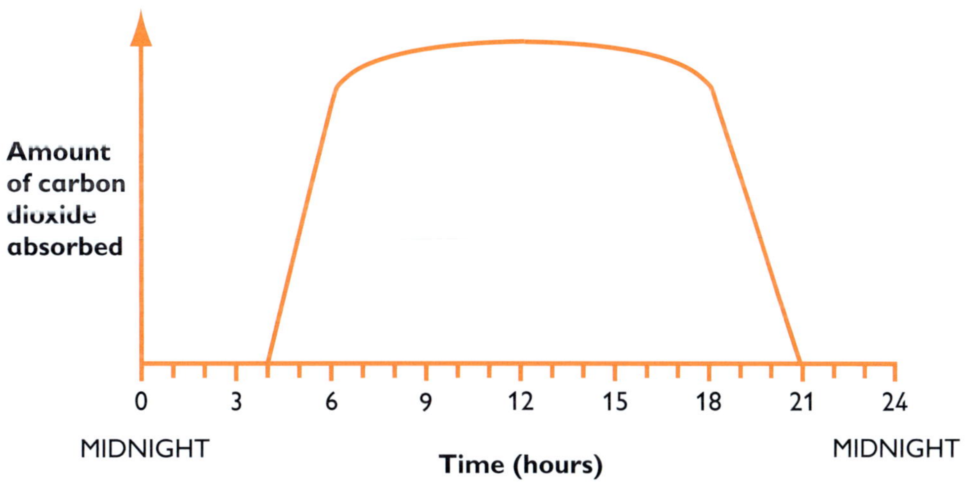

TOTAL

5

At what time did the Sun rise?

1

Explain your answer.

2

c Name **two** substances produced in photosynthesis.

_______________ and _______________

2

d Describe **two** ways in which the rate of photosynthesis could be increased.

i

ii

2

TOTAL

7

10 A ray of **red** light falls on a glass prism as shown in the diagram.

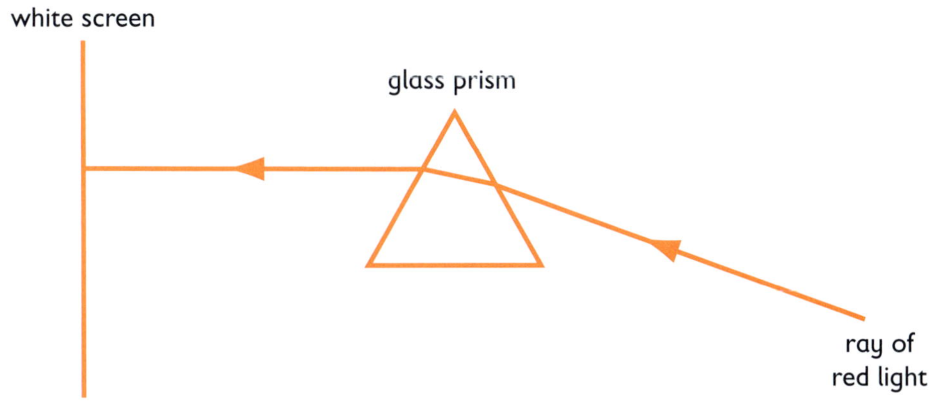

a A blue filter is placed between the prism and the screen.

i What would you now see on the screen?

____ 1

ii Explain how the blue filter causes this effect.

____ 2

b The red ray is replaced by a ray of white light.

i What would you now see on the screen with the blue filter still in place?

____ 1

ii What would you see on the screen if the blue filter was removed?

____ 1

TOTAL 5

Circuits

11 Anna connects a battery and a switch to an electric bell as shown.

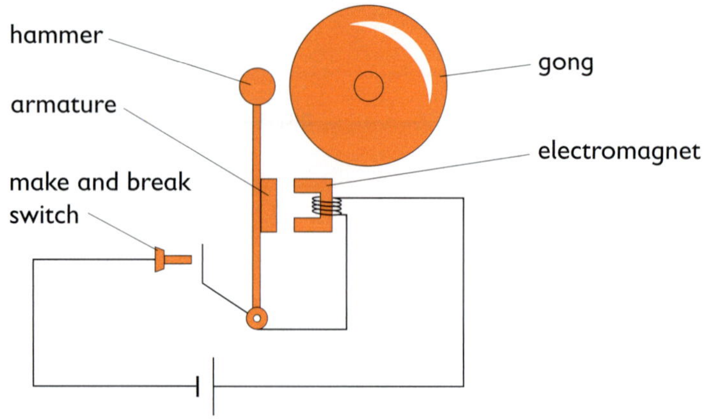

a When Anna closes the switch, what will happen to the armature?

1

b Explain how the movement of the armature switches off the electromagnet.

2

c The electromagnet has a metal core.
Name a suitable metal for this core.

1

d Describe **two** ways in which the strength of the electromagnet in the bell could be increased.

2

TOTAL

6

12 The table below shows the chemical formulae of six substances.

Substance	Chemical formula
table salt	$NaCl$
limestone	$CaCO_3$
potassium chloride	KCl
malachite	$CuCO_3$
bauxite	Al_2O_3
silver	Ag

a From the table, give the name of **one** substance which is:

i a metallic element ______________________ 1

ii a metallic oxide ______________________ 1

iii a compound containing copper ______________________ 1

iv a compound containing chlorine ______________________ 1

v a carbonate ______________________ 1

TOTAL 5

b The diagrams represent the way atoms are arranged in some of the gases found in air. Each atom is represented by a circle. The atoms are labelled with their chemical symbols.

1 

2 

3 

4 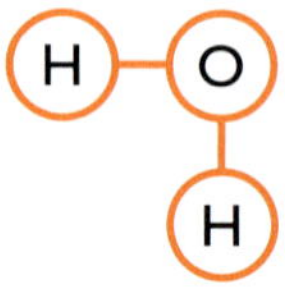

i Which **two** diagrams represent the structure of chemical elements?

________________ and ________________

2

What are the names of these elements?

________________ and ________________

2

Which **two** diagrams represent the structure of chemical compounds?

________________ and ________________

2

ii Name one gas found in air that is not shown above.

____

1

c Iron reacts with one of the gases shown in part **b** to form rust.

i What is the name of this type of reaction?

____

1

ii Write a word equation for this reaction

iron + ____________ → ____________

2

TOTAL

10

13 The diagram shows David and Marie playing on a seesaw.

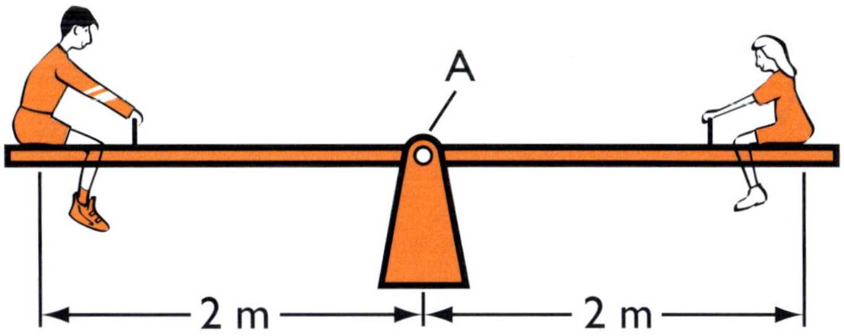

a What is point A called?

____

1

b David's body applies a moment (turning effect) to the seesaw. David weighs 400 N. Calculate the size of the moment created by his weight. Give the units.

____

2

c Marie weighs 200 N. Calculate the size of the moment created by her weight. Give the units.

____

2

d Calculate where David will have to sit on the seesaw to make sure that both moments are equal.

____

2

TOTAL

7

Acids and alkalis

14 The table shows the pH of different water samples taken from five lakes.

Water sample	pH
A	8.0
B	7.0
C	6.0
D	7.5
E	4.0

Use letters from the table to answer the questions below.

a Which water sample is the most acidic?

1

b Which water sample is neutral?

1

c The water from one of the lakes is too acidic to allow fish to live. Lime is an alkaline substance and could be added to the lake to reduce the acidity.
What type of reaction takes place between acid and lime?

1

d Part of the reactivity series is given below.

sodium
magnesium
aluminium
zinc
iron
copper
gold

TOTAL 3

i Write down the name of **one** metal from the series that will react violently with acids.

____ 1

ii Write down the name of **one** metal from the series that will not react with acids.

____ 1

iii Explain why containers for acids cannot be made from iron or steel.

____

____ 1

e Some magnesium ribbon is placed into a test-tube containing some copper sulphate solution.

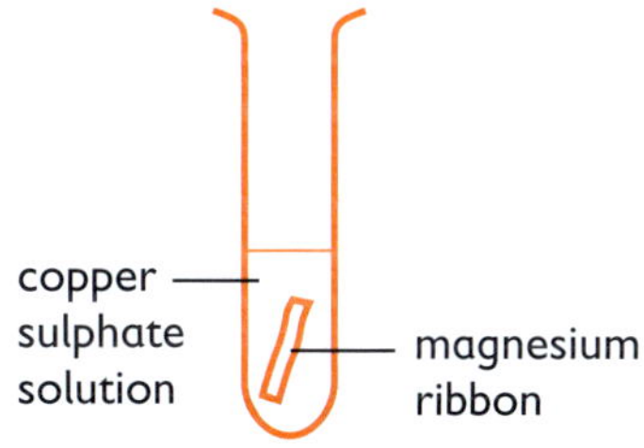

i Describe what happens to the magnesium ribbon.

____ 1

ii Describe what happens to the copper sulphate solution.

____ 1

iii Explain why this change takes place.

____

____ 2

TOTAL 7

Magnets

15 The diagram below shows an investigation into the strength of an electromagnet. The results of the investigation are given in the table.

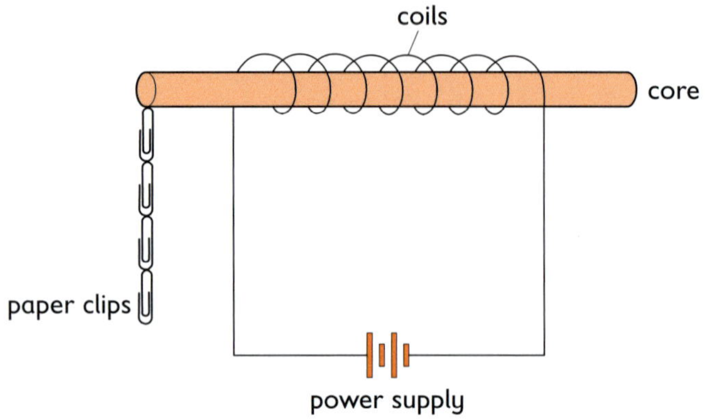

Number of coils	Number of paper clips
0	0
5	1
10	3
15	4
20	6
25	7
30	8

a On the graph paper below draw a graph of the results.

4

TOTAL

4

b What is the relationship between the number of coils and the number of paper clips?

____

____

1

c Predict the number of paper clips that could be attracted if the number of coils was increased to 40.

____

1

d List **two** other factors that could be changed to affect the strength of an electromagnet.

i ______________________________ 1

ii ______________________________ 1

e Write down **two** ways in which you could make sure that the testing of the strength of an electromagnet is carried out as a fair test.

i ______________________________ 1

ii ______________________________ 1

TOTAL

6

END OF TEST 2

Answers

Test 1

Question number	Answer	Mark	Comments and tips
TEST 1			
1a	light	1	
1b	i. air ii. iron iii. Metals are good conductors of sound. Sound will travel through metals many times faster than through air.	1 1 2	
2a	cell B Plant cells have a cell wall/a vacuole; animal cells do not.	1 1	One reason needed.
2b	1 = cell membrane 2 = cytoplasm 3 = nucleus 4 = cell wall 5 = chloroplast 6 = vacuole	6	
2c	Plant cells have chloroplasts, a vacuole and a cell wall.	2	Two answers needed.
2d	producers	1	
2e	Their chloroplasts contain chlorophyll, which captures light energy.	2	
3a	i. insect ii. fly larvae, eel/small fish iii. small fish/newt, large fish	5	
3b	heron, kingfisher, otter, beetle, eel, small fish, newt or large fish	1	One answer needed.
3c	The number of beetles is likely to increase.	1	
3d	The number of small fish is likely to decrease because their food supply (beetles) will diminish.	2	
4a	Those in Experiment 2 ✓	1	
4b	water/temperature/amount and type of soil	2	Two factors needed.
4c	So that the amount of light is the only variable.	1	
4d	The more plants used, the more reliable the results would be.	2	
4e	Height of plants. The colour of their leaves.	2	
4f	The leaves of the plants in Experiment 1 will be yellow. The plants in Experiment 2 will be taller.	2	
5a	i. kettle, tea pot *or* cup/saucer ii. water iii. steam from the kettle	3	One mark per answer.
5b	A liquid has a definite volume. A gas takes the shape of the container. A solid is not able to flow.	3	
5c	density	1	
5d	A – melting B – freezing/solidifying C – vaporisation/evaporation D – condensation	4	
6a	B – no C – yes D – no E – no	4	
6b	i. copper wire, steel nail, aluminium foil ii. paper, plastic spoon	5	
7a	Arrow A should start at the front of the sledge and point to the child's hand.	1	
7b	Arrow B should start at the child's hand and point to the front of the sledge.	1	
7c	It will speed up.	1	
7d	Arrow C should point downwards from the middle of the sledge.	1	
7e	i. Arrow A should point vertically downwards. ii. Arrow B should point vertically upwards.	2	A parachutist falls at a constant speed when the air resistance is an equal and opposite force to gravity.
8a	in the east	1	
8b	in the west	1	
8c	noon	1	
8d	The Earth spins on an axis through its poles as it orbits the Sun so the Sun appears to move.	1	

Question number	Answer	Mark	Comments and tips
8e	i. B ii. C iii. A iv. D	4	One mark per correct answer.
9a	Component 1, bulb. Component 2, switch.	2	
9b	A	1	
9c	Yes, because closing the component (switch) completed the circuit.	3	
10a	carbohydrates, vitamins or water	2	
10b	i. For growth and to repair damaged tissue. ii Any two from: making energy, making/repairing cell membranes, helping to protect organs, insulating the body. iii. An excess of fat can make you obese and can clog your arteries, causing circulation problems. iv. scurvy	2 2 2 1	
11a	skull	1	
11b	ribs	1	
11c	It consists of many sections – vertebrae – which allow it to bend.	1	
11d	i. triceps ii. biceps iii. The arm muscles work in pairs to produce movement – one works in the opposite way to the other.	1 1 2	Muscles that work in pairs are called antagonistic muscles.
12a	wood, sand or plastic	1	
12b	salt or sugar	1	
12c	soluble	1	
12d	i. smaller particle size/pieces ii. stir the mixture iii. use hot water	3	
13a	i. sand ii. water iii. A = filter funnel, B = filter paper, C = filtrate	1 1 3	
13b	i. green ink ii. purple ink iii. yellow ink *or* red ink *or* blue ink	3	One mark per correct answer.
14a	They will repel.	1	
14b	They will attract.	1	
14c	Attracted: iron, steel. Not attracted: copper, plastic	4	
14d	Select two from: fridge magnets, door closings, games, loudspeakers, lifting, compasses, electric bells	2	
15a	i. anther ii. ovary iii. stigma	3	One mark per correct answer.
15b	Pollen is made in the **anther**. This pollen can be spread to other flowers by **wind** and **animals**. When the pollen lands on the flower it can stick to the **stigma**. A pollen tube then grows down the style into the **ovary**.	5	
16a	as potential energy	1	
16b	potential energy	1	

National Curriculum Levels

Mark	0–36	37–75	76–96	97–112	113–125
Level	Below Level 3	Level 3	Level 4	Level 5	Level 6

If your child needs more practice in any Science topics, use the WHSmith Key Stage 3 Science Revision Guide.

Answers

Test 2

Question number	Answer	Mark	Comments and tips
TEST 2			
1a	A = cell wall D = chloroplasts B = cytoplasm E = vacuole C = nucleus	5	
1b	The root. Root hair cells do not contain chloroplasts as they are not exposed to sunlight.	3	One mark for identifying the part; two marks for a complete explanation.
1c	Any two from: chloroplasts vacuole cell wall	2	
1d	Any two from: nerve, muscle, skin, lung	2	
1e	A red blood cell is full of the pigment haemoglobin, which takes up oxygen from the lungs and distributes it to the body's cells.	2	
2a	The heart	1	
2b	Circulatory system	1	
2c	The second box down should be ticked.	1	
2d	i. It transports materials around the body. ii. It allows the exchange of materials from blood to cells.	2	
3a	Plant A had had more light so was able to make more food.	2	
3b	Two from: Each plant must have an equal amount of water. The temperature must be the same. The type of soil must be the same.	2	
3c	With more plants they could check for consistency of results and their conclusion would be more reliable.	2	
4a	Both salts become more soluble as the temperature increases, but to a different extent.	1	
4b	potassium nitrate	1	
4c	40 g per 100 cm^3 of water	1	
4d	60 g	1	
4e	0°C	1	
4f	i. Stir the mixture. ii. Use smaller pieces of the salts.	2	
5a	A = lava C = magma chamber B = sill D = dyke	4	
5b	Liquid to solid.	1	
5c	Rocks at B.	1	
5d	i. sedimentary ii. Dead sea creatures with shells sink to the bottom of the sea. Layers form and solidify into rock. iii. metamorphic iv. High temperatures are needed for marble to form. Point X is near to a large area of hot rock. Point Y is only near a small area, which cools faster. v. Limestone (sedimentary). It is formed from layers of animal and plant remains. Also, the other rocks are heated and squashed.	1 2 1 2 2	
6a	C	1	
6b	angle of incidence	1	
6c	B	1	
6d	incidence, equal, reflection	3	
6e	Light will leave the mirror at the same angle as it hits it – therefore to see themselves the person must be in front of the mirror.	1	
7a	acid	1	
7b	i. hydrogen ii. Put a lighted splint into the gas – it will go "pop" if the gas is hydrogen.	1 2	
7c	i. carbon dioxide ii. Collect it and bubble it through limewater – $Ca(OH)_2(aq)$ – it will turn the limewater cloudy.	1 2	
8a	many possible, including: pond plants → snails → small fish pond plants → insects → small fish microscopic plants → larvae → snails	3	
8b	pond plants or microscopic plants	1	
8c	Predator: small fish Prey A: insects Prey B: snails	3	
8d	Decrease, because the larvae would have less food so fewer will survive.	2	
8e	C	1	

Question number	Answer	Mark	Comments and tips
9a	cell wall – helps to keep the shape of the cell nucleus – controls the cell's activities cytoplasm – a place where many chemical reactions take place chloroplast – photosynthesis takes place here cell membrane – controls substances entering and leaving the cell	5	
9b	4 a.m. The plant started to photosynthesise and absorb carbon dioxide at that time.	3	
9c	Food *or* sugar *or* glucose and oxygen	2	
9d	Increase the amount of light. Increase the amount of carbon dioxide.	2	Photosynthesis requires light and water.
10a	i. Nothing. ii. The blue filter absorbs all the red light.	1 2	
10b	i. Blue light only. ii. A rainbow.	1 1	Filters absorb all colours but their own.
11a	It will be attracted to the electromagnet and move towards it, making the hammer hit the gong.	1	
11b	The movement of the armature opens the switch, which turns off the current.	2	
11c	Iron	1	Iron loses its magnetism quickly when the current is switched off.
11d	By increasing the voltage and increasing the number of coils in the electromagnet.	2	
12a	i. silver ii. bauxite iii. malachite iv. table salt or potassium chloride v. malachite or limestone	5	One mark per correct answer.
12b	i. 2 and 3 oxygen and argon 1 and 4 ii. nitrogen	2 2 2 1	
12c	i. oxidation ii. iron + oxygen $\rightarrow$ iron oxide	1 2	Iron reacts with the oxygen in air and water to form rust.
13a	pivot *or* fulcrum	1	
13b	800 Nm	2	Moment = weight x distance from fulcrum (= 400 N x 2 m)
13c	400 Nm	2	Moment = weight x distance from fulcrum (= 200 N x 2 m)
13d	1 m from the pivot	2	
14a	E	1	
14b	B	1	
14c	neutralisation	1	The lime is a base, which reacts with the acid to form a salt and water.
14d	i. sodium ii. gold iii. Because these metals react with acids (to produce a metal salt and hydrogen).	3	One mark per correct answer.
14e	i. It changes into a reddish-brown solid. ii. Its blue colour fades. iii. Magnesium is higher than copper in the reactivity series, so it displaces the copper from the copper sulphate.	1 1 2	
15a	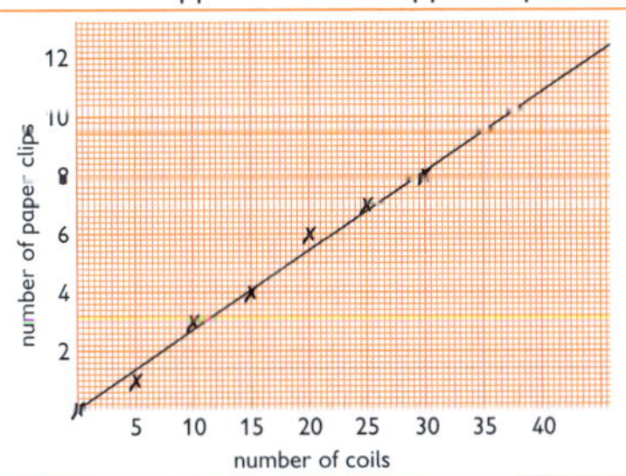	4	2 marks for correctly labelled axes, 1 mark for plotted points, 1 mark for best-fit line.
15b	The greater the number of coils, the greater the number of paper clips attracted.	1	
15c	11 paper clips	1	
15d	Use a soft iron core that is horseshoe-shaped with coils on each arm. Increase the electric current.	2	
15e	Only alter one variable at a time. Use a constant electricity supply.	2	

National Curriculum Levels

Mark	0–39	40–80	81–105	106–123	124–135
Level	Below Level 4	Level 4	Level 5	Level 6	Level 7

If your child needs more practice in any Science topics, you could use the WHSmith Key Stage 3 Science Revision Guide.

Extension Paper

(Level 8)

Attempt this test if you have scored highly on Tests 1 and 2.

Atoms

1 The diagram shows a sodium atom.

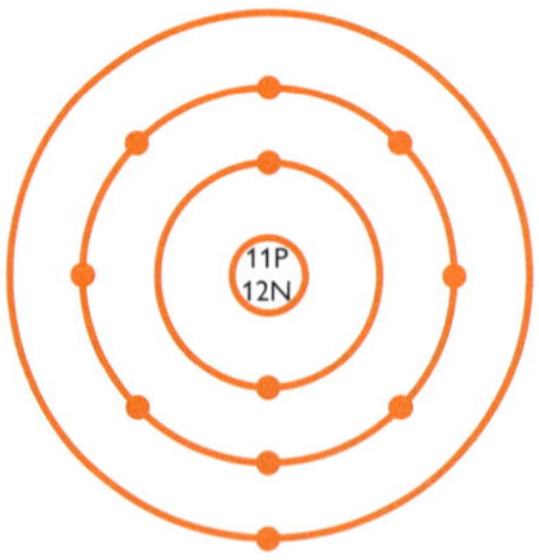

a How many protons are there in a sodium atom? ______________ 1

b What is the atomic number of sodium? ______________ 1

c The electronic pattern for sodium can be shown as 2, 8, 1.
Complete the following table. 6

Element	Number of electrons	Number of protons	Atomic number	Electronic pattern
He^{4}_{2} helium	2			
C^{12}_{6} carbon		6		
F^{19}_{9} fluorine			9	
K^{39}_{19} potassium				2, 8, 8, 1

d What is the name of the compound formed from potassium and fluorine? 1

____

e What is the formula for this compound? 1

____

TOTAL

10

2 Abdul did an experiment to find out the relative reactivities of four metals. Small pieces of the metals were placed in dilute solutions of different salts. Some of the results are shown below.

	Reaction			
	Magnesium in copper sulphate	**Iron in copper sulphate**	**Magnesium in zinc sulphate**	**Zinc in iron sulphate**
Colour of metal at start	silver	dark grey	silver	light grey
Colour of metal at end		brown	light grey	
Colour of solution at start	pale blue	pale blue	colourless	pale green
Colour of solution at end		pale green	colourless	

a Use the information in the table to complete the **four** missing sections. 4

b Use the information in the table to identify:

i the most reactive metal 1

___

ii the least reactive metal 1

___

c Use the information to predict what would happen if a piece of copper was added to zinc sulphate. 1

___

d Write a word equation for the reaction between magnesium and zinc sulphate. 1

___

TOTAL 8

3a Match each word to its correct definition.

A	dominant	1	A section of nucleic acid of a chromosome responsible for a particular characteristic
B	genotype	2	The outcome of a particular gene
C	recessive	3	Always expresses itself
D	gene	4	Symbols representing the alleles present for a particular gene
E	phenotype	5	Works only when partnered by another like itself

5

b The colour of some flowers is controlled by a pair of alleles, R (red) and W (white). A cross between a pure-bred red flower and a pure-bred white flower produces just red flowers.

i Write down the alleles for flower colour in the following:

The pure-bred white flower

_______________________________________ 1

The pure-bred red flower

_______________________________________ 1

ii Complete the diagram to show how two plants with red flowers can produce red-flowering plants and white-flowering plants. 8

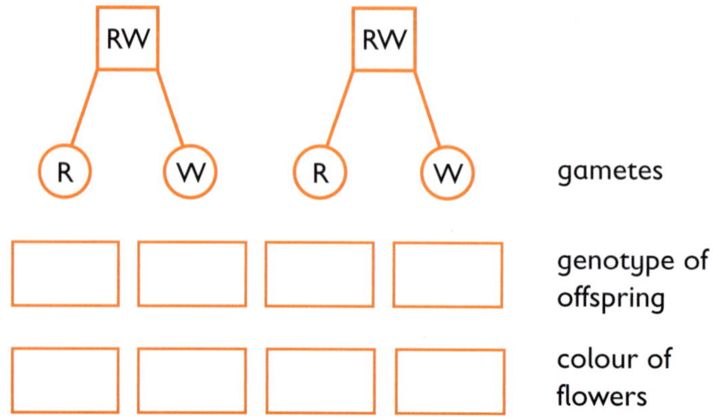

TOTAL

15

4a There are two forms of cell division: **meiosis** and **mitosis**. The table below shows information about cell division. For each statement on the left, tick the correct box.

	Meiosis only	**Mitosis only**	**Both types of division**
Number of chromosomes in the cell is halved			
Replaces worn out body cells			
Occurs only in reproductive organs			
Genetic material is copied before cell division			

4

b Explain why the cells produced by mitotic division are genetically identical to each other.

1

c Explain **two** ways in which sexual reproduction can give rise to variation in the offspring.

2

TOTAL

7

END OF EXTENSION PAPER

Extension Paper
Answers

Question number	Answer	Mark	Comments and tips
EXTENSION			
1a	11	1	
1b	11	1	The atomic number is the number of protons (= number of electrons) in the atom.
1c	2 2 2 2 6 6 6 2, 4 9 9 9 2, 7 19 19 19 2, 8, 8, 1	6	$\frac{1}{2}$ mark per correct answer.
1d	potassium fluoride	1	
1e	KF	1	
2a	reddish-brown black colourless colourless	4	
2b	i. magnesium ii. copper	2	One mark per correct answer.
2c	no reaction	1	
2d	magnesium + zinc sulphate → magnesium sulphate + zinc	1	
3a	A – 3 B – 4 C – 5 D – 1 E – 2	5	One mark per correct answer.
3b	i. WW RR ii. RR RW RW WW red red red white	2 8	One mark per correct answer.
4a	meiosis only mitosis only meiosis only both types of division	4	One mark per correct answer.
4b	The new (daughter) cells' chromosomes are replicas of the parent cells' chromosomes.	1	
4c	The offspring inherit genes from both parents so are different from their parents. Mutations can mean that cells are given the wrong genetic information and so work differently.	2	Two answers needed.

National Curriculum Levels

Mark	0–20	21–40
Level	Below Level 8	Level 8